BODY SYSTEMS

Thinking and Feeling

Angela Royston

Heinemann

First published in Great Britain by Heinemann Library
Halley Court, Jordan Hill, Oxford OX2 8EJ
a division of Reed Educational and Professional Publishing Ltd.

OXFORD FLORENCE PRAGUE MADRID ATHENS MELBOURNE
AUCKLAND KUALA LUMPUR SINGAPORE TOKYO IBADAN
NAIROBI KAMPALA JOHANNESBURG GABORONE
PORTSMOUTH NH (USA) CHICAGO MEXICO CITY SAO PAULO

© Reed Educational and Professional Publishing Ltd 1996

Designed by Inklines and Small House Design
Illustrations by: Gary Rees: p.4, p.9, p.20 (right), p.22; John Bovosier: p.8; Peter
Bull Art Studio: p.12, p.14, p.16, p.20 (left), p.24, p.27; Frank Kennard: p.10.
Printed in Great Britain by Bath Press Colourbooks, Glasgow
Originated in Great Britain by Dot Gradations, Wickford

00 99 98 97 96
10 9 8 7 6 5 4 3 2 1

ISBN 0 431 06208 0

British Library Cataloguing in Publication Data
Royston, Angela
    Thinking & feeling. – (Body systems)
    1. Thought and thinking – Juvenile literature
    2. Perception – Juvenile literature 3. Touch – Juvenile literature
    I. Title
    612.8'2

Acknowledgements
The Publishers would like to thank the following for permission to reproduce
photographs:
Barnaby's Picture Library: p.4; Corbis/Bettmann: p.7 (bottom); Image Bank:
p.13; "PA" Photo Library (Press Association/Topham): p.5; Sally and Richard
Greenhill: p.15 (bottom); Science Photo Library: p.9, p.15 (top), p.21, p.27,
p.28, p.29; Telegraph Colour Library: p.25; Tony Stone Images: p.6, p.7 (top),
p.11 (both), p.17 (both), p.18, p.23, p.26.

Commissioned photograph p.19: Trevor Clifford.
Cover photograph: Trevor Clifford.

Our thanks to Yvonne Hewson and Dr Kath Hadfield for their comments in
the preparation of this book.

Every effort has been made to contact copyright holders of any material
reproduced in this book. Any omissions will be rectified in subsequent
printings if notice is given to the Publisher.

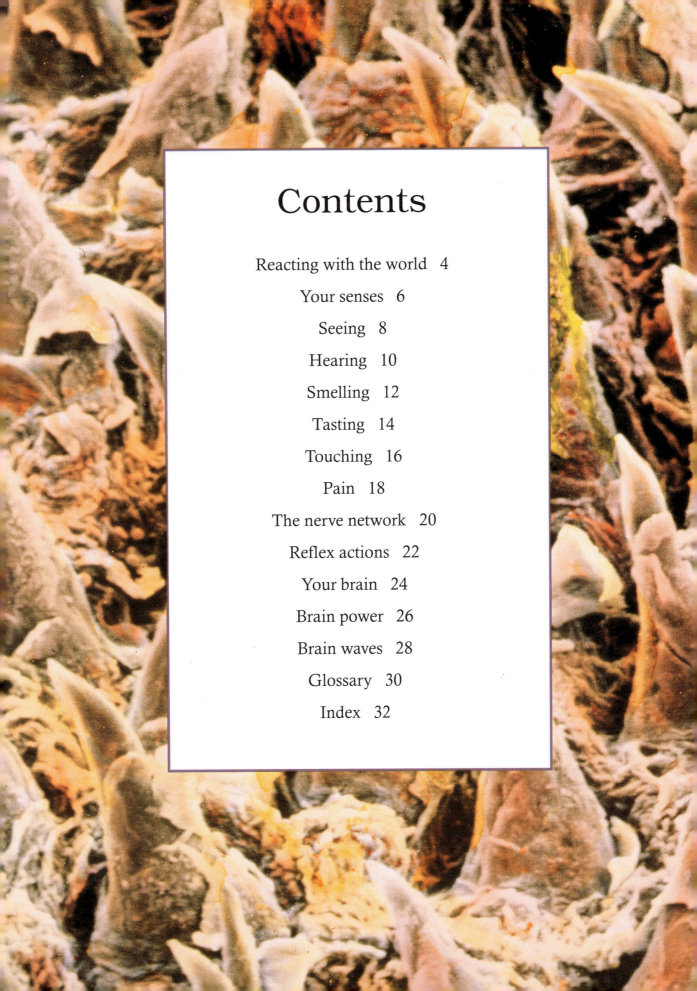

Contents

Reacting with the world

Imagine what it would be like if, all of a sudden, you could neither see nor hear. You could not cross the street alone safely because you would not see or hear the traffic. Eyes and ears are two of your five **sense organs**. They send messages along your **nerves** to your **brain**. Your brain controls your whole body and it is more complicated and powerful than any computer. It interprets messages from your sense organs and tells your **muscles** and **glands** how to respond.

Your nervous system

Your sense organs, nerves and brain form your body's main communication system, called the **nervous system**. Nerves are like fine electrical wires which carry signals from the **senses** to the brain and from the brain to the muscles. The brain itself is a soft lump made of millions of **nerve cells**, connected together in countless different ways.

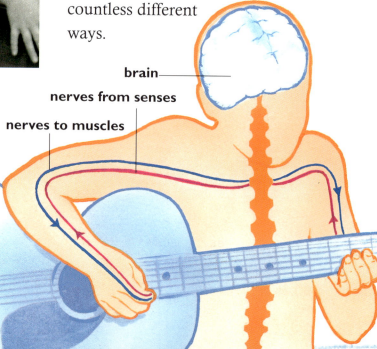

brain

nerves from senses

nerves to muscles

▲ *This girl is using her senses and her brain as she plays the guitar. She feels the strings with her fingers and she hears the sounds they make with her ears. Her brain interprets the sounds she hears as notes and tells her fingers what to do.*

▶ *Nerves carry messages to the brain from the senses and from the brain to the muscles telling them to act.*

◄ You use your brain for everything you do and feel. When you are watching a football match, your brain interprets signals from your eyes to tell you what is happening and it makes you feel excited, pleased or disappointed at what you see.

Your brain

Your brain is responsible for everything you think, feel and know. Even many high-powered computers working together could not do what your brain does. You can plan ahead, you can decide whether something is good or bad, and you experience many different emotions, including happiness, anger and excitement. Your brain receives information from your sense organs and continuously sends messages to your body.

You are not aware of everything that your brain does. It controls all the other systems in your body. For example, it triggers the muscles that you use to breathe air in and out of your **lungs**, so that even when you are fast asleep, you continue to breathe. It controls every aspect of your **digestive system** – the muscles that push food through the intestines and the glands that make digestive juices. It also controls your liver, kidneys and other internal organs.

Did you know?

Your body is made up of billions of tiny cells. Muscles, bones, blood, skin, nerves and so on are each built of a different kind of cell. Nerve cells are different shapes and sizes. The nerve cells in the brain are the smallest kind of cell in the body.

Your senses

How do we discover the world around us? Even as newborn babies, we begin to explore the things near to us through our **senses**. A baby soon recognizes its mother's face or father's voice. But sight and hearing are just two of your five senses. The other three are smell, taste and touch. Between them they tell you everything you know about the world. Your senses gather information which your **brain** then processes and uses.

Gathering information

Your eyes, ears, nose, tongue and skin are **sense organs**. They have special **receptors** which detect a particular **stimulus**. Receptors in your eyes detect light. Those in your ears detect sound waves. Tiny chemical **particles** activate smell and taste. Receptors in your skin and deep inside your body pick up heat, cold, pressure and pain. When they are stimulated, they send **electrical signals** along your **nerves** to your brain.

Bombarded with information

Your senses bombard your brain with information all the time. Your brain quickly interprets the incoming signals and ignores the unimportant ones. Although you can hear the noise of traffic outside, you probably don't notice it until, perhaps, a fire engine races by with its siren blaring. You can feel the pages of this book, but you probably notice other things touching your body only if they make you uncomfortable.

▶ *The girls eating these pieces of orange can see, smell and taste them. They can also feel the orange in their hands and the sticky juice on their lips.*

Co-ordination

Your senses work together to help you do what you want to do. You can see where something is, but the sense of touch helps you to pick it up. Your brain becomes so quick at co-ordinating the senses and **muscles** that you do many things without thinking about them. When you first start to play a new computer game, you have to learn how the keys affect what is happening on the screen. After a while the links between your senses of sight, sound and touch, your brain and the keys become automatic and you play the game without thinking about the keys.

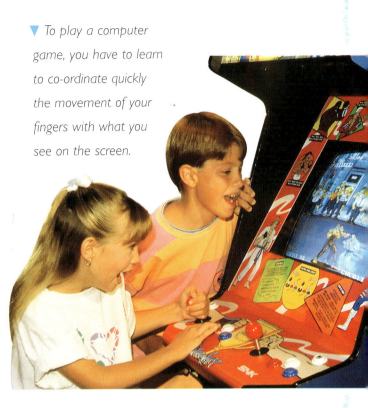

▼ To play a computer game, you have to learn to co-ordinate quickly the movement of your fingers with what you see on the screen.

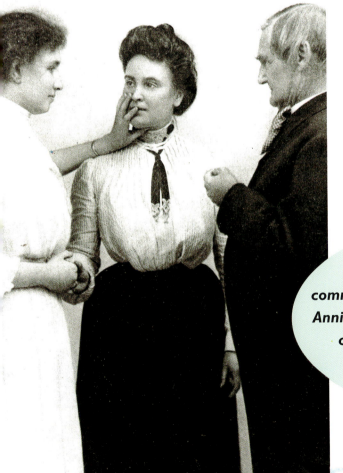

◄ Helen Keller became blind and deaf before she had learned to speak, so she could not imitate the sounds of speech. Instead she put her hand over her teacher's lips and throat and learned to copy the movement and vibrations she felt.

Did you know?

Helen Keller could not talk or communicate with anyone until a teacher, called Annie Sullivan, taught her to communicate using only the sense of touch. Annie slowly and patiently taught Helen to read **Braille** and even to speak.

Seeing

Your eye works rather like a camera. The black circle in the centre is a hole called the pupil. It is covered by a transparent window called the cornea. Light enters your eye through the cornea and the pupil. It then passes through the lens which focuses it so that a clear but upside-down 'picture' forms on the retina at the back of your eye. **Nerve endings** in the retina send the picture to your **brain**.

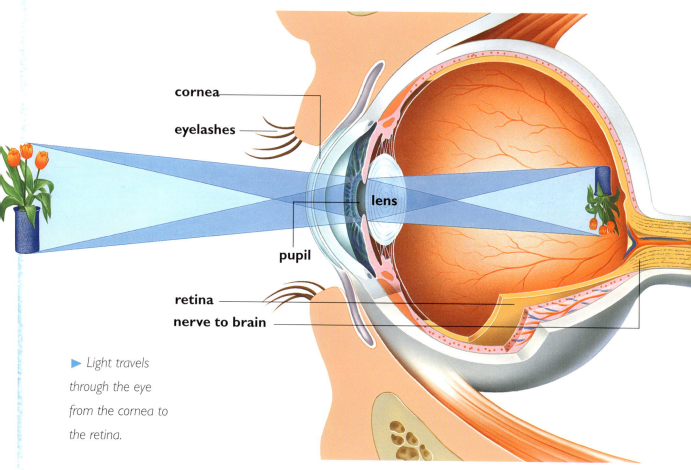

cornea

eyelashes

lens

pupil

retina

nerve to brain

▶ Light travels through the eye from the cornea to the retina.

Colour or black and white?

The back of the retina is lined with two kinds of **light-sensitive cells** called rods and cones. Cones detect different colours but only work well in bright light. Rods work best in dim light but don't detect colour.

That is why everything looks grey or black in dim light. When light falls on rods and cones, it triggers **electrical signals**. These pass from the nerve endings along the nerve fibres to the optic nerve, which takes them to your brain.

Learning to see

Although we say that a picture is formed on the retina, it is not a picture like a photograph. What the brain receives is a changing pattern of electrical signals, like those that make a picture on your television screen. The brain interprets the signals to make the picture that you see.

Babies must learn to 'see'. They first recognize simple patterns, then slowly learn to distinguish more complicated shapes and colours. Blind people who regain their sight also have to learn to make sense of the world around them.

▲ If you look at this drawing one way, it looks like two faces. If you look at it another way, it looks like a vase. Your brain can make sense of this picture in two different ways.

Did you know?

The retina makes colour pictures rather like a TV screen does. Some cones react only to red light, others only to blue or to green. Every other colour is a combination of these three. Some people are 'colour blind'. Either their cones do not work properly or there is something wrong with the nerve to the brain. Either way, they cannot tell all the colours apart, particularly red and green. More boys than girls suffer from some colour blindness – about 8 in every 100.

Hearing

If you bang a drum you can hear a sound. You might also feel the drum quivering, or vibrating. The air around it vibrates too, creating invisible sound waves. They spread out, like ripples on a pond. Some of the sound waves reach your ears and pass down the ear canal to the eardrum. They then travel through your ear to the **nerves** that send signals to your **brain**.

Journey through the ear

The outer ear is the part you can see. It is a flap of skin and **cartilage** which picks up sound waves. These make your eardrum vibrate. The eardrum divides the outer ear from the three bones of the middle ear. These pick up vibrations from the eardrum and magnify them. From the middle ear, sound waves pass through the oval window into the inner ear. Here is found the cochlea, a spiral tube which is filled with liquid. Inside it, **nerve cells** pick up vibrations in the liquid, sending **electrical signals** along the auditory nerve to the brain. Your brain interprets the signals as sound.

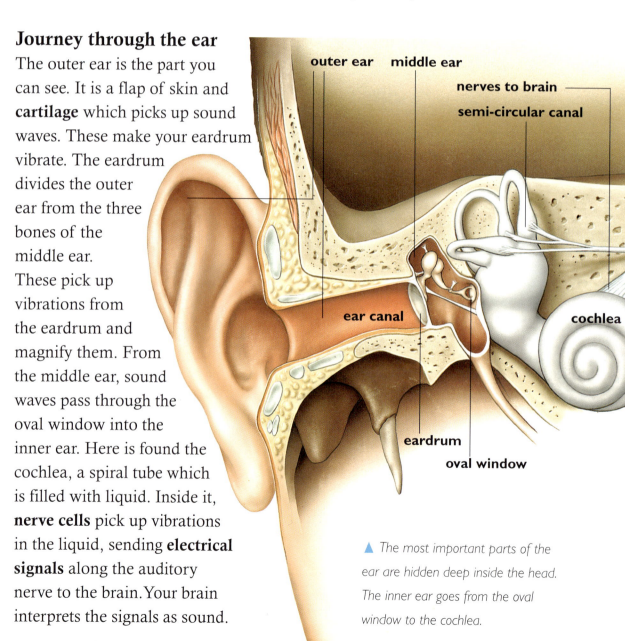

outer ear   middle ear

nerves to brain

semi-circular canal

ear canal

cochlea

eardrum

oval window

▲ The most important parts of the ear are hidden deep inside the head. The inner ear goes from the oval window to the cochlea.

Balancing act

The inner ear also contains three semicircular canals. These three tubes are at right angles to each other and they help your sense of balance. They are filled with liquid so every time you move, the liquid in the semicircular canals moves too. **Nerve endings** in the canals send messages to the brain. In this way you know what position your body is in because your brain knows how the liquid in the semicircular canals is moving.

▲ *Your sense of balance tells you which way up you are. The liquid inside this boy's semicircular canals tells him that he is upside-down.*

▶ *Loud noises can damage the delicate workings of the ear. This worker is wearing earmuffs to protect his ears from the noise of the drill.*

Did you know?

The loudness of sound is measured in decibels. A whisper is only about 30 decibels, and a loud alarm clock is about 80. Road drills can reach 100 decibels but jet planes can reach an ear-splitting 140 decibels. Noises over 90 decibels can damage your hearing, and those over 165 decibels can even kill you.

Smelling

We rely most on sight and hearing to tell us about the world, but smell is very important too. Bad smells tell us that some things, such as rotting food, can harm us. What you smell are gases in the air, tiny floating **particles** that you breathe into your nose. When you want to smell something better, you sniff because this takes more particles to the smell-detecting **cells**.

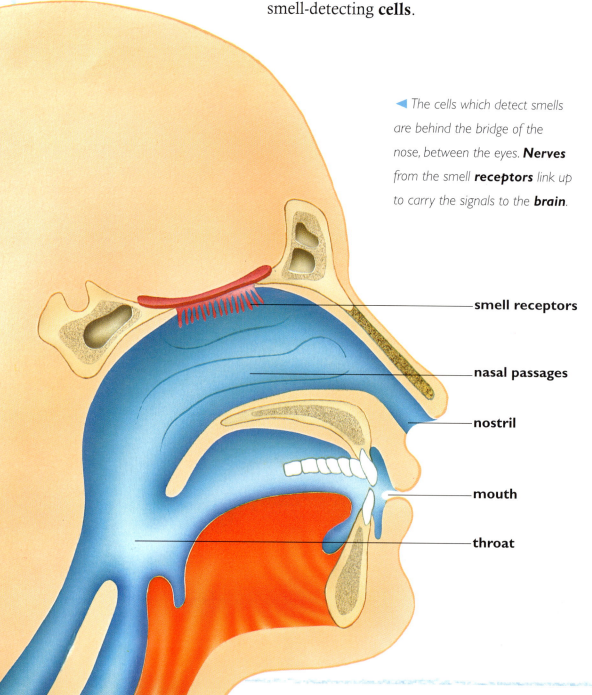

◀ The cells which detect smells are behind the bridge of the nose, between the eyes. **Nerves** from the smell **receptors** link up to carry the signals to the **brain**.

smell receptors

nasal passages

nostril

mouth

throat

Inside the nose

Your nose is bigger than you think. It stretches back into the head above the mouth. The two nostrils lead to nasal passages made by three pieces of bone. The nostrils and nasal passages are lined with **mucus** and tiny hairs which catch any dirt and germs. Smell receptors are sunk in a layer of mucus and only detect particles which have dissolved in it.

Too much mucus, however, destroys the **sense** of smell. If you have a cold and your nose is blocked, no particles can get through the mucus to the smell receptors, and so you cannot smell anything. The sense of taste relies heavily on the sense of smell. Much of what you think is taste is really smell, so, if you can't smell, you cannot taste much either.

Smell and memory

Smells are often very closely linked with memory. The smell of suntan oil, for example, may make you think of last summer's holiday. The part of the brain which deals with smell is very close to the part which deals with memory. In fact, messages about smell pass through the memory area of the brain on their way to the smell area.

◀ *Bad smells, like those from rotting rubbish, warn us of possible danger.*

Did you know?

There are about 5 million smell receptors at the top of each nostril. No one knows exactly how the brain tells one smell from another. Human beings can in fact detect over 3000 different smells, but many animals can do much better. A dog's sense of smell is over a million times more sensitive than ours. Dogs can track people from the smell of their footprints!

Tasting

Most of us do not have a very good **sense** of taste. Some people, such as chefs, can recognize many different tastes in just one mouthful of food. But most people cannot even tell an apple from a pear if they shut their eyes and block their nose. The **cells** which detect taste are in the mouth, mainly on the tongue. The tip and edges of the tongue are covered with taste-buds which are each sensitive to one of four basic tastes – salty, sweet, sour and bitter. Every taste is either one or a combination of these.

▼ *Different parts of the tongue detect mainly one kind of taste.*

bitter

sour

sour

salt

salt

sweet

Your tongue

The surface of your tongue is rough and moist. The roughness comes from tiny **papillae**. Taste-buds in the papillae detect chemicals dissolved in saliva. Saliva, with food dissolved in it, flows through the opening of the taste-bud and **stimulates** the taste cells inside. When the taste cell is triggered, an **electrical signal** passes down the **nerves** to your **brain**. Somehow your brain puts together the signals from all the taste cells and produces the sense of taste.

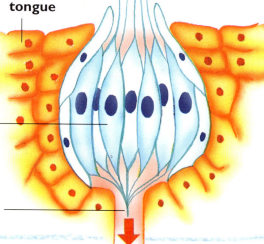

tongue

taste cells

nerve to brain

► *This taste-bud has been enlarged thousands of times.*

◀ The surface of the tongue magnified over 335 times. This shows what a rough surface your tongue has.

Enjoying food

Your sense of taste alone is not very strong. It is helped by all the other senses. Think of a food you really like, pizza perhaps. The sight and smell of one makes your mouth water. As you bite into it, the smell increases. The sound of the chewing and the feel of the pizza in your mouth all add to the pleasure of eating. Humans like the taste of sweet things from the moment they are born, but we don't usually like the taste of very bitter things.

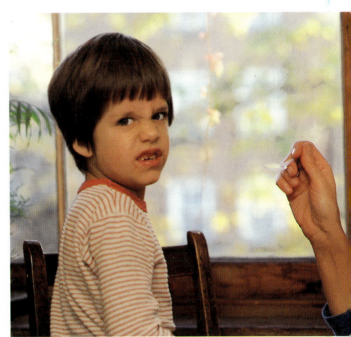

▲ Medicine is good for you, but it often tastes bitter. Some medicines are sweetened to make them taste more pleasant.

Did you know?

If you look in the mirror and stick out your tongue, you will see a V-shaped row of papillae at the back of the tongue. These not only detect bitter tastes, they also help to protect you from poisons. If a taste is very bitter they trigger the 'gag' reflex. You automatically spit out the bitter substance. You can't rely on the gag reflex, however: some poisons taste sweet.

Touching

Unlike the other **senses**, the **receptors** which respond to touch are found throughout your body, mainly in your skin. There are several kinds of touch receptor. Some **nerve cells** in the skin react to heat, some to cold, others to touch, pressure and pain.

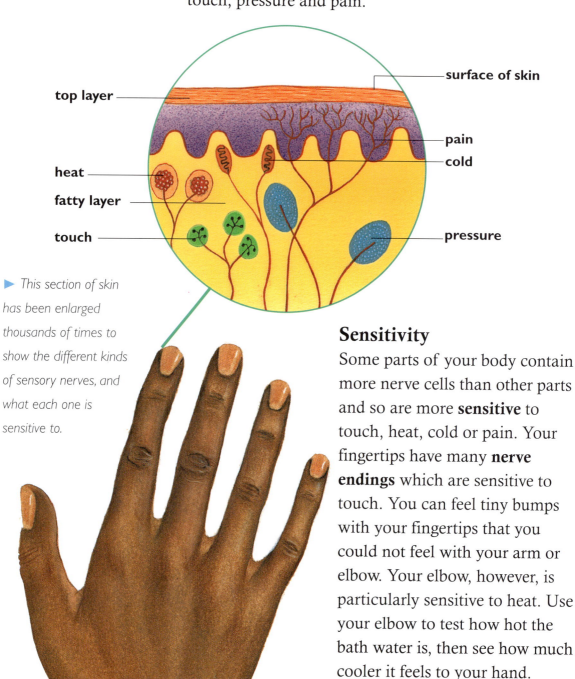

top layer

surface of skin

pain

cold

heat

fatty layer

touch

pressure

► This section of skin has been enlarged thousands of times to show the different kinds of sensory nerves, and what each one is sensitive to.

Sensitivity

Some parts of your body contain more nerve cells than other parts and so are more **sensitive** to touch, heat, cold or pain. Your fingertips have many **nerve endings** which are sensitive to touch. You can feel tiny bumps with your fingertips that you could not feel with your arm or elbow. Your elbow, however, is particularly sensitive to heat. Use your elbow to test how hot the bath water is, then see how much cooler it feels to your hand.

◄ The sense of touch is important to all of us. Simply stroking a pet makes us feel more relaxed and happy.

▼ When you touch something, you may feel more than one sensation. For example, these icicles feel cold, smooth and heavy.

Your lips and tongue are sensitive to touch, heat and cold. You test food with your lips to make sure it won't burn your mouth. And have you noticed that when a tooth falls out, the gap left feels enormous to your tongue? Your back, however, has many fewer touch receptors. If someone touches you lightly on the back, you may not even feel it.

'Seeing' by feeling

Blind people tend to develop their sense of touch and use it instead of sight to find their way around. They use their fingers to feel objects around them and a stick to 'feel' the pavement in front of them. **Braille**, the special alphabet of raised dots which allows blind people to read, is read by touch through the fingertips.

Did you know?

The very top layer of skin is dead. It consists of hard, tough cells that protect the living cells below. New skin cells are made in the lower layers and are slowly pushed up towards the surface. Old, dead cells rub off against your clothes and when you wash. In fact much of the dust in your house is made up of dead skin cells!

Pain

There are many more pain **receptors** than other kinds of **nerve endings** in the skin. So it is easier to say exactly where a pain is than where a feeling of pressure is. Pain is useful in telling you when something is wrong, but some people seem to feel pain more strongly than others. There are several kinds of pain. Pain receptors near the surface of the skin make you feel tickly or itchy. Those lower down give a stabbing pain, but if pain receptors deeper still are triggered, you feel a dull, throbbing ache.

▶ Some doctors use **acupuncture** instead of an anaesthetic to stop their patients feeling pain during an operation. The patient then stays awake throughout the operation. Acupuncturists are specially trained so they know exactly where to place the needles.

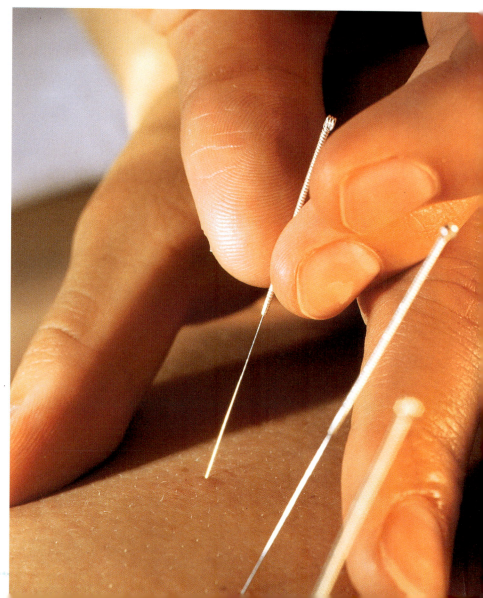

◀ *Unexpected pain makes you cry out in shock. It also makes you more careful next time!*

A useful warning

If you fall and hurt yourself, you usually feel pain. Pain stops you walking or running on a damaged ankle or leg, so the injury has time to heal. But the amount of pain does not necessarily show how bad the damage is. The prick of a thorn can be agonizing, while a deep cut may hardly hurt at all. Lepers know how important the feeling of any kind of pain is. Leprosy is a disease which can damage the nerve endings so that the person does not feel pain. Lepers are often injured because they don't notice when something is burning or hurting them.

Deadening pain

Anaesthetics deaden or lessen pain. Some act on a part of the body (local anaesthetic), some on the whole body (general anaesthetic). A local anaesthetic acts on particular nerve endings and connections. Footballers and other athletes sometimes use local anaesthetics to numb pain during a game so that they can go on playing. A general anaesthetic makes a patient unconscious during an operation so that they feel no pain and are not aware of the operation.

Did you know?

Some people train themselves not to feel pain, or to overcome the feeling of pain in the mind. Yogis in India lie on beds of nails and walk through fire. You can help yourself control pain without doing anything so dangerous. Fear can make pain feel worse. The next time you have an injection, try to relax and not pull away from the pain. If you can do this, it should be less painful.

The nerve network

There are different kinds of **nerves**. Sensory nerves collect information from the **senses**, and **motor nerves** pass messages between the **brain** and every other part of your body. The **sense organs** have **nerve endings** which produce **electrical signals** when they are **stimulated**. The signal passes from one **nerve cell** to another along the nerve to your brain. A fine network of nerves spreads out from the brain, through the **spinal cord** and all over your body.

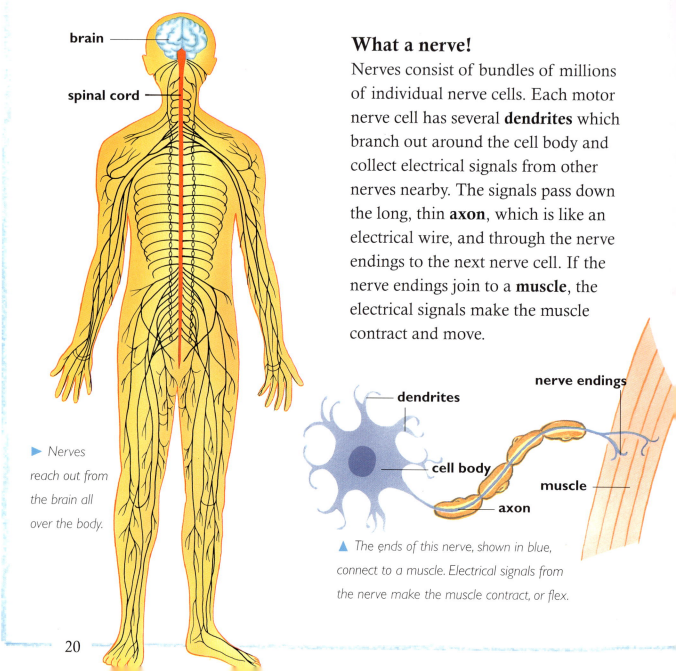

brain

spinal cord

▶ Nerves reach out from the brain all over the body.

What a nerve!

Nerves consist of bundles of millions of individual nerve cells. Each motor nerve cell has several **dendrites** which branch out around the cell body and collect electrical signals from other nerves nearby. The signals pass down the long, thin **axon**, which is like an electrical wire, and through the nerve endings to the next nerve cell. If the nerve endings join to a **muscle**, the electrical signals make the muscle contract and move.

nerve endings

dendrites

cell body

muscle

axon

▲ The ends of this nerve, shown in blue, connect to a muscle. Electrical signals from the nerve make the muscle contract, or flex.

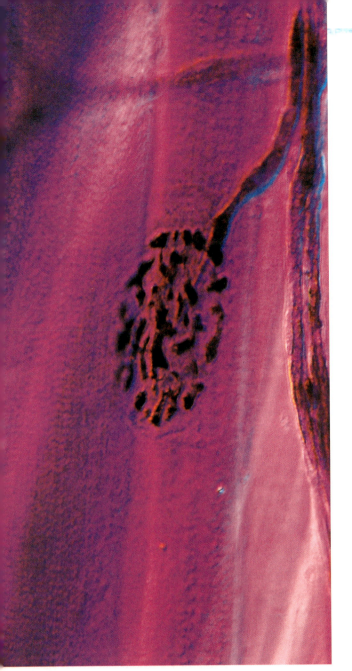

The spinal cord

Twelve pairs of nerves leave the brain and connect directly with the eyes, ears, mouth, nose, neck and vital organs, such as the heart. The main highway for nerves to the rest of the body is the spinal cord. It is protected by a column of bones – the vertebrae that make up your spine. Pairs of nerves leave the spinal cord and split into smaller and smaller branches until they reach all over your body.

Paralysis

If the spinal cord is injured, then parts of the body may become paralyzed. The sensory nerves' messages can no longer get through and link with the muscles. How much of the body is paralyzed depends on how far up the spine the injury is. If the bottom of the spine is hurt, only the legs will be affected. If the injury is to the neck, however, then most of the body may be paralyzed.

▲ A single motor nerve cell magnified hundreds of times. It conducts electrical signals from the brain to the muscle.

Did you know?

Bare electrical wires are very dangerous to touch. They are usually insulated with a plastic covering. Similarly some nerve axons have an insulating covering. Usually, it is only the end of the nerve that needs to be sensitive – the rest of the nerve simply carries the message from the nerve endings to the brain.

Reflex actions

Have you ever noticed that if you prick your finger, you pull it away even before you've noticed the pain? This is called a **reflex action**. The body acts fast, without waiting for the **brain** to realize what is happening. The **nervous system** can respond so quickly because some signals from the sensory **nerves** are relayed directly to the **motor nerves** in the **spinal cord** bypassing the brain. The motor nerves go into action while the rest of the signals travel on to the brain.

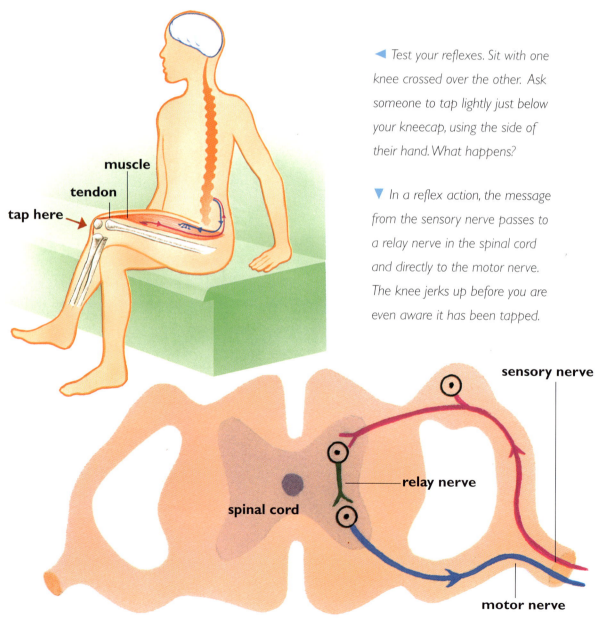

◀ *Test your reflexes. Sit with one knee crossed over the other. Ask someone to tap lightly just below your kneecap, using the side of their hand. What happens?*

▼ *In a reflex action, the message from the sensory nerve passes to a relay nerve in the spinal cord and directly to the motor nerve. The knee jerks up before you are even aware it has been tapped.*

muscle

tendon

tap here

sensory nerve

relay nerve

spinal cord

motor nerve

Knee-jerk reactions

Sit with one leg crossed over the other and ask someone to tap your leg just below the kneecap. When they tap the right spot, your knee will jerk upward of its own accord. This is just one of many reflex actions you are born with. Blinking if something comes close to your eyes is also a reflex action, and so is sneezing. If something tickles the inside of your nose it can be very hard to avoid sneezing. Swallowing is another reflex action. When a mouthful of food reaches the back of your throat, you automatically swallow it.

Working unawares

Some reflexes work without you even being aware of them. They are controlled by a special part of the brain and are called the **autonomic nervous system**. When you move from dim light to bright light, the pupil of your eye closes to stop too much light entering the eye. When you are hot, the tiny blood vessels near the surface of the skin stretch so that more blood is brought to the surface to be cooled. Other parts of your body, such as your heart, **digestive system** and kidneys, also work without you being aware of them.

▶ As these athletes get hot, their autonomic nervous system cuts in to help keep them cool.

Did you know?

Electrical signals travel much more slowly along the nerves than along electric wiring. Copper wiring carries electrical signals almost as fast as the speed of light (300,000 km per second). The fastest nerve messages, such as those that make you blink, travel at only 120 m per second, but they don't have far to go, so we don't usually notice any delay. The slowest signals, such as those that carry pain messages from your toes to your brain, may travel at only 1m per second.

Your brain

Your **brain** is a soft lump which looks like a huge wrinkled walnut. It is in fact a complex network of **nerve cells** supplied with blood. The blood feeds the nerve cells. Your whole brain is encased in a watery cushion which helps to protect it from bumps and bangs. Outside this is a thick covering of bone, (the skull), skin and hair. The brain is divided into different parts, each with its own job to do.

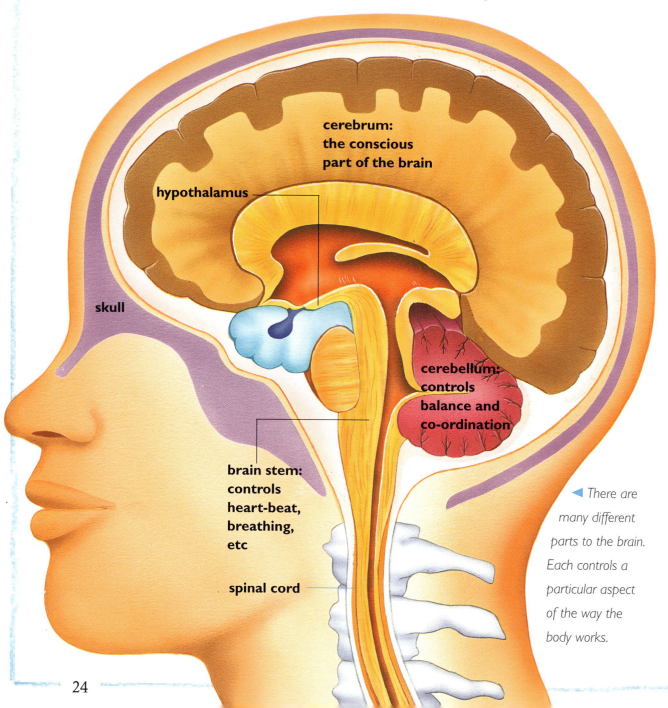

cerebrum: the conscious part of the brain

hypothalamus

skull

cerebellum: controls balance and co-ordination

brain stem: controls heart-beat, breathing, etc

spinal cord

◄ *There are many different parts to the brain. Each controls a particular aspect of the way the body works.*

Cerebrum and cerebellum

The largest part of your brain is the **cerebrum**. This wrinkled mass makes up four-fifths of the whole and it controls everything you are aware of, such as thinking, remembering and moving. It also processes information from your **senses**. The rest of the brain is hidden beneath the cerebrum. The **cerebellum** controls balance and co-ordinates messages to the **motor nerves** so that all our movements are smooth and controlled.

Brain stem

The **brain stem** controls the body systems that keep you alive, such as your breathing, **digestion** and heart-beat. Special nerves, which form the **autonomic nervous system**, leave the brain stem and go directly to your heart and to the **muscles** which control digestion and breathing. These messages do not normally reach the cerebrum, so you are not usually aware of them.

At the top of the brain stem is the **hypothalamus**. It controls the temperature of your body and links to feelings such as thirst, hunger, anger and pleasure. Strangely, the nerves cross over in the brain stem, so that the left side of your brain controls the right side of your body, and the right side of the brain controls the left side of your body.

◀ These athletes are sweating and pushing their muscles to their limit. Their brains control their bodies and minds – they are determined to keep running and beat the other competitors.

Did you know?

At the centre of the brain stem is a message filter called the reticular formation. It acts as a watchdog for the rest of the brain. It filters all the messages coming from the spinal cord and allows only the most important ones to reach the cerebrum. This saves you having to think about unnecessary information.

Brain power

The **cerebrum** consists of two large domes each covered by a folded, wrinkled layer of **nerve cells** called the **cortex**. The cortex contains all the thoughts and feelings that we are aware of. It allows us to reason, plan ahead and use language. Human beings have a bigger cortex than any other animal, which is why we are more intelligent. The cortex also processes and interprets information from the **senses** and controls the **muscles**. Each of the senses is controlled by a particular area of the cortex.

◀ *Playing chess involves complicated calculation and planning ahead. Both of these are controlled by the area at the front of the cortex.*

Touch and movement

The part of the cortex which deals with the sense of touch forms a band across the cortex. Messages from the touch **receptors** come here. The parts of the body which have a lot of touch receptors take up a larger area of the cortex. The lips and the fingers have the largest areas of all.

Next to the sensory area on the cortex is the motor area. It receives messages from the **sense organs** and sends out commands to the muscles. The fingers and mouth, which use many different muscles, take up a larger area of the cortex than other parts of the body.

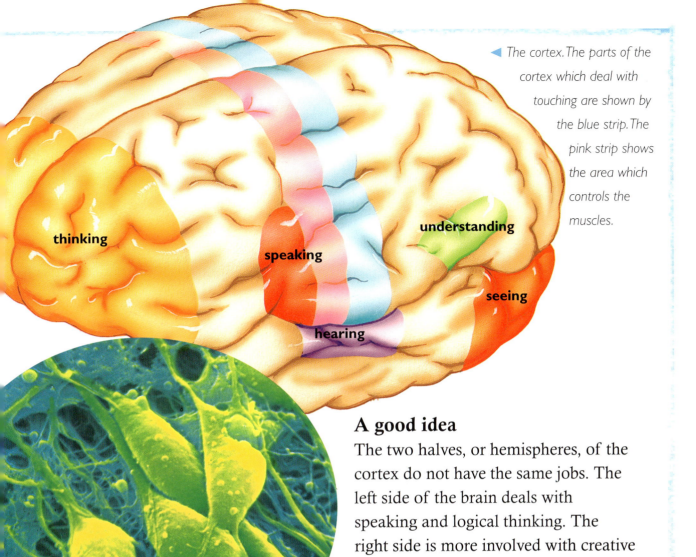

The cortex. The parts of the cortex which deal with touching are shown by the blue strip. The pink strip shows the area which controls the muscles.

thinking

speaking

understanding

seeing

hearing

Nerve cells in the brain look like a tangled mess, but they form pathways which allow us to learn, remember and control our lives.

A good idea

The two halves, or hemispheres, of the cortex do not have the same jobs. The left side of the brain deals with speaking and logical thinking. The right side is more involved with creative and artistic pursuits. We all use both sides of the brain, but most people are governed more by the left side, and like to reason out a solution to a problem. People who usually jump to an answer using their intuition probably prefer to use the right side of their brain.

Did you know?

The folds on the cortex give extra room to cram in more brain cells – 100,000 million altogether. Each one is connected to at least 50,000 others, giving the human brain an immense capacity for learning and remembering. Unlike other cells in our body, brain cells cannot renew themselves. They die off slowly as we grow older.

Brain waves

There is still much about the **brain** that scientists do not understand. It is difficult for them to study the brain, but they can record and study brain waves – the electrical activity of the brain. Electric wires can be lightly attached to the head. They pick up **electrical signals** in the brain and relay them to machines called electro-encephalographs. The machine displays the signals as an electro-encephalogram (EEG), irregular lines shown on a screen or on paper.

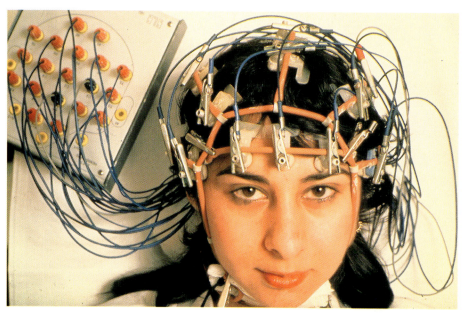

◄ *An electro-encephalograph is measuring and recording the electrical signals in this girl's brain. The machine can help to detect some illnesses and to study sleep and dreams.*

Dreams

You may think you do not dream very much, but scientists have discovered that most people have about five dreams a night. They know this because they have studied the EEGs (that is, they have studied the brain waves) of people when they are asleep. At the same time they measured the movement of their eyes and how tense their muscles were.

When you dream, the EEG changes pattern and your eyes move very fast. Dreams change to non-dreaming sleep then back to dreams. You are most likely to remember a dream if you wake up in the middle of it. No one knows why we dream. Some dreams seem to be about the day's events. Other dreams may express our secret wishes and fears.

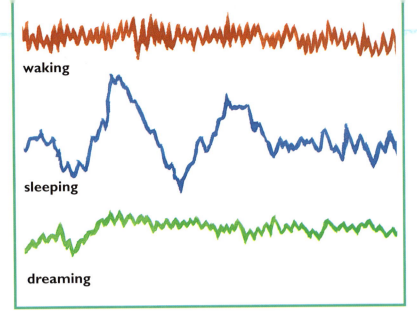

waking

sleeping

dreaming

◄ *The machine prints out rows of jagged lines called an electro-encephalogram (EEG). These 'brain waves' form different patterns according to whether the person is alert, relaxing, thinking, asleep or dreaming.*

Brain death

At one time a person was said to have died when their heart stopped beating. But today machines can often restart the heart. If someone stops breathing for more than four minutes, the brain becomes starved of oxygen and brain **cells** begin to die. Even so, the person may still be alive. As long as the **brain stem** keeps working, the body stays alive, even though the person is not aware (conscious). It is only when the brain stem fails that the person is really dead.

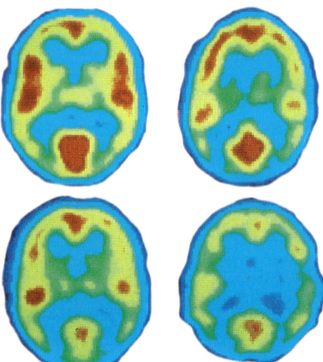

▲ *These brain scans or PET (pultron emission tomography) scans are a kind of X-ray of the brain. The red areas show which parts of the brain are working.*

Did you know?

When you are dreaming your muscles are totally relaxed. Have you ever had a nightmare when you couldn't run or scream no matter how you tried? Your muscles were too relaxed to respond! Sleep-walking and talking happen during non-dreaming sleep. The sleeper's eyes may be open, but they cannot see. And when they wake up they cannot remember anything about it.

Glossary

Acupuncture A system of medicine which treats illness and pain by putting small needles into the patient's skin at very particular points of the body.

Autonomic nervous system The part of the nervous system that controls things that happen in your bodies without you being aware of them. For example, it controls the different muscles which keep your heart beating and your lungs breathing and which push food through your digestive system.

Axon The long, thin extension of a nerve cell which sends electrical signals away from the cell.

Braille A system which uses raised dots to represent each letter of the alphabet. Blind or partially sighted people can feel the dots with their fingers and so read the words.

Brain A large mass of nerve cells which controls most of the workings of the body. The brain is situated in the head and is protected by the skull. It receives information through the senses and sensory nerves, and it controls the muscles through the motor nerves.

Brain stem Part of the brain that controls the autonomic nervous system.

Cartilage A smooth but tough gristle. It covers the ends of bones to protect them, and is also found in the ear flaps and at the end of the nose. It is firm but bendy.

Cell The building block of all living things, including your body. Each part of your body – skin, bone and so on – consists of millions of microscopic cells. Each kind of cell looks different and does a particular job. For example, nerve cells carry electrical signals, usually to or from your brain.

Cerebellum Part of the brain, beneath the much larger cerebrum. The cerebellum controls balance and co-ordination.

Cerebrum The largest part of your brain. It forms a dome over the rest of the brain and its nerve cells deal with messages from the senses, thinking, memory, talking and all the things that you are aware of.

Cortex The outer, folded and wrinkled layer of nerve cells in the two domes that make up the cerebrum.

Dendrite A branched projection from a nerve cell body.

Digestive system The digestive system is a long tube that stretches from the mouth through the stomach and intestines to the anus. It breaks down food in the body into small particles that can be absorbed into the blood.

Electrical signals Tiny pulses of electricity. They are carried to and from the brain by nerve cells. Electrical signals also pass from one part of the brain to another. We experience these electrical signals as light, sound, taste, thought, memory and feeling.

Gland An organ of the body which makes substances such as hormones or digestive juices.

Hypothalamus The top of the brain stem. It controls body temperature and links with feelings such as thirst, hunger, anger and pleasure.

Insulated Cut off from surroundings by a protective covering. Electrical wires are insulated with plastic to stop electricity leaking out. The axons of some nerve cells are similarly insulated with fatty cells.

Light-sensitive See **Sensitive**.

Lungs The parts of the body which take oxygen from the air into the blood and release carbon dioxide from the blood back into the air. The lungs are in the chest and air is breathed in and out through the nose or mouth.

Motor nerves Nerves that pass messages between the brain and the muscles or glands.

Mucus A thick liquid which lines many of the inner surfaces of the body. It keeps them moist and traps germs.

Muscles Bundles of fibres which have the ability to contract (shorten) and relax. There are three types in our bodies. The most obvious are those that are attached to bones. They move our arms and legs.

Nerve A bundle of millions of nerve cells which passes electrical signals to and from the brain. Each nerve cell detects a stimulus when the stimulus reaches a certain level.

Nerve cells See **Cell**.

Nerve ending The end of a nerve. In the sense organs nerve endings detect a particular kind of stimulus by sending an electrical signal along the nerve to the brain. For example, nerve endings in the skin react to pain, pressure, heat or cold.

Nervous system The body's communication system. It links the body and the brain. It carries information from the senses to the brain and commands from the brain to the muscles. The autonomic nervous system controls the muscles which work without us thinking about them.

Papilla (plural papillae) A small raised part of the skin, for example on the tongue or finger tip, in which a nerve ends.

Particle Small part of something. The smallest part of a substance that can exist by itself is called a molecule. Molecules of gas stimulate the sense of smell and molecules of food stimulate the sense of taste.

Receptors Nerve cells in the sense organs that react to a stimulus, such as light, sound or pressure, by generating an electrical signal. See also **Nerve ending**.

Reflex action Rapid action by the body as the nervous system responds to a message from sensory nerves that is relayed to motor nerves in the spinal cord.

Sense organs Parts of the body, such as the eyes, ears, tongue, nose and skin, which receive information from the outside world. The sense organs consist of groups of nerve cells which detect particular stimuli, such as light, sound, chemical particles or touch, and which send electrical signals to the brain.

Senses The five senses are sight, hearing, smell, taste and touch. The sense organs inform the brain of changes in the environment. The brain interprets the signals from the sense organs so that we experience sight, sound, smell, and so on.

Sensitive Able to react to a stimulus.

Spinal cord Bundles of nerve cells protected by the backbone. The spinal cord carries sensory and motor nerves. Messages pass along it from the senses to the brain and from the brain to the muscles. Relay nerves in the spinal cord sometimes link a sensory nerve directly with a motor nerve to produce a fast, reflex action.

Stimulus Something which triggers a reaction or response.

Index